SPECIAL MINISTERS

OF THE EUCHARIST

William J. Belford

A PUEBLO BOOK

The Liturgical Press   Collegeville, Minnesota

Nihil Obstat:
Daniel V. Flynn, J.C.D.
Censor Librorum

Imprimatur:
✠ Joseph T. O'Keefe
Vicar General, Archdiocese of New York
March 23, 1984

Design: Frank Kacmarcik

The publisher gratefully acknowledges the generosity and hospitality of the parish of the Sacred Heart, Suffern, New York, where the photographs for this book were taken.

Printed in the United States of America

ISBN 0-8146-6039-8

Contents

Introduction

Ministers are people entrusted to perform a special function for the members of their community. As the Catholic Church, a community of faith and love, continues to change under the vision and reforms of the Second Vatican Council, we are growing in appreciation and utilization of many kinds of ministries.

In some instances, we are restoring ministries that we once had, such as the ordained ministry of the diaconate. In other instances, we are on the verge of officially recognizing the services of people like catechists and cantors who have been working faithfully without formal commission or blessing. And in some instances, under the guidance of the pope and bishops, we are creatively defining new ministries in response to proliferating needs.

One of these new ministries is that of helping priests and deacons in the distribution of holy communion, either at Mass, or at another time, when the eucharist is carried to the homebound or hospitalized. The people who do this are called *special ministers of the eucharist*.

This booklet is an effort to help our community better understand and implement this ministry. As a resource, it is intended for study by special ministers themselves, so that they will perform their service with skill, sensitivity, and satisfaction.

I. Eucharistic Ministry in the Church

By the grace of baptism and incorporation into the Church, Catholic Christians are called to live generous lives of prayer and service. We are to serve the needs of one another as an expression of our shared life and our love for God, who has saved us in Jesus Christ.

There are many ways open to us to render this service, and they are not mutually exclusive. Some possibilities are: helping in matters of social welfare, assisting in the work of Christian education, contributing to the support of the church, and taking ministerial roles in the celebration of our public worship.

For many centuries, this fourth category has not been included in the list of available options, as an ordained clergy was given prime responsibility for liturgical ministry. The lay people were thus relegated to an almost passive role in the liturgy. Since, however, all baptized Christians share the common priesthood of the faithful, we all have the potential for taking significant responsibility for the public worship of our community.

It was this potential that was ignored for many centuries, contrary to the ordinary practice of the early Church and the theology expressed in the First Letter of Saint Peter. That epistle emphasized the inherent dignity of baptized people and addressed the Christian people as "a chosen race, a royal priesthood, a holy nation, a people God claims for his own. . . . Once you were no people, but now you are God's people (2.9-10).

This loving kindness from our God invites a loving response from all his people. As members of his Church we are acknowledging now, more than in our recent history, that ministry is a universal obligation, conditioned by the community's needs, our abilities, and the call of the Lord.

This theology of the priesthood of the faithful and of diverse ministries is liberating, in that it frees us from former conventions, and encourages us to use our talents for the Church. But it is still relatively new to us, and many people may be hesitant to take on responsibilities, especially in the area of eucharistic ministry. To dispel any such hesitation, we can look to the practices of the early Church and Catholic teaching about the eucharist.

THE EARLY CHURCH AND THE EUCHARIST

In the first centuries of the Church's existence, we know that members of the community were accustomed to carry the eucharist home with them and to give it to their relatives and friends who were ill and could not be present at the Sunday assembly. Since Mass was not celebrated every day, they even kept the eucharist in a safe place and received it on other days during the week. This ministering of the eucharist to one another by members of the laity is an important part of our tradition which shows us that holy communion was customarily handled by the faithful during the early centuries of the Church.

The early Church is our model in many ways for our ideas about the eucharist and the Mass. We picture the early Christians as gathering together for the Sunday Mass, with many ordained ministers present: a celebrant (frequently enough, the bishop of the area), his assistant priests, and deacons. Thus when it was time to distribute holy communion, there ordinarily would have been a sufficient number of ordained ministers to see that everyone received without undue delay.

The people, of course, received holy communion under both forms, bread and wine, taking the bread and then the chalice into their own hands when it was given to them by the minister. Since this was the ordinary procedure, there probably would have been no special concern if other people were called upon to distribute the bread or hand the cup to one another on occasions when there was an insufficient number of ordained ministers. There is, however, no evidence that such was the case. The important point is that the laity in the early Church did handle the eucharist and did take it to the sick.

In the United States, most dioceses have made use of the permission to implement the option of allowing the faithful to receive holy communion in their hands, and then to put it in their own mouths, and to take the chalice into their own hands and drink from it. In preparation for the introduction of communion in the hand, we were given some examples from our history that showed that centuries ago, as now, there was a concern for propriety and respect for the eucharist.

For instance, Origen, one of the great Fathers of the Church, warned that a person who takes the body of the Lord in his hands must do so with caution, so that nothing would be lost. St. John Chrysostom made a connection between the manner of reception and the state of the soul:

"Tell me, would you go to the eucharist with your hands unwashed? I think not. You would rather not go at all than go with dirty hands. If you are so careful about a small matter, how can you dare to go and receive the eucharist with an impure soul? With your hands you hold the Lord's body only a short time, but it remains in your soul forever."

St. Cyril of Jerusalem, completing his instructions to people who had just been baptized, gave them a now-famous lesson in eucharistic etiquette:

"When you approach communion, do not come with your hands outstretched or with your fingers open, but make your left hand a throne for the right one, which is to receive the King. With your hand hollowed receive the Body of Christ and answer Amen. After having, with every precaution, sanctified your eyes by contact with the holy body, consume it, making sure that not a particle is wasted, for that would be like losing one of your own limbs. Tell me, if you were given some gold dust, would you not hold it very carefully for fear of letting any of it fall and losing it? How much more careful then you should be not to let fall even a crumb of something more precious than gold or jewels! After having received the Body of Christ, approach the chalice of his Blood. Do not stretch out your hands, but bow in an attitude of adoration and reverence, and say Amen."

While there is general agreement that all the people of the Church—priests, deacons, and laity—received the Lord in their hands as the normal custom for the first nine centuries of the Church's life, there is also an awareness that a different kind of spirituality and practice dominated the Church for the next ten centuries, right up to the time of the Second Vatican Council (1962–65). To treat this question briefly, we may note that about the ninth century, complicated social, theological, and disciplinary considerations led to the abolition of the practices of lay people receiving the Lord in their hands, drinking from the communion cup, and taking the eucharist to the sick.

Factors which contributed to this refusal to entrust the eucharist to the laity included a rise in superstitious attitudes about the consecrated bread (e.g., some people took the eucharist home and preserved it as a good luck charm). As a reaction to such abuses, a eucharistic theology arose which demanded very reverent respect for the Blessed Sacrament. There was simultaneously an increased emphasis on the privileged position of the clergy, with a consolidation of other people's ministries into theirs and a general tightening-up of church discipline.

The result of all this was a major change in eucharistic spirituality. Receiving the wafer-host on the tongue became the norm; common bread was no longer used as it had been in the past. People were not offered the chalice to drink the precious blood. Members of the congregation received less often, as they were constantly reminded of their unworthiness. Respect for the sacrament replaced hunger for it, adoration and awe took the place of participation and communion.

This was the basic mindset the church lived with for almost a thousand years. The Mass was thought of as a sacred drama that Christians had to "hear and see," rather than as a celebration that they participated in. People were considered to be very presumptuous if they received holy communion more than a few times a year. "Confession before communion" became the rule. The reluctance to receive was so great toward the end of this period that a "law of the church" was written to require Catholics to go to holy communion at least once during the year. Even in the early years of our century, first holy communion was often delayed until children had become teenagers. As late as 1910 in some places, the usual age for first communion was fourteen.

In that year, Pope Pius X published an encyclical entitled *Quam Singulari*. He desired to change the pattern that kept people away from holy communion, and so he specifically encouraged frequent communion and set the age of reason as the proper time to introduce children to the sacrament of the eucharist.

In the decades that followed, children began receiving at about the age of seven, but people were only gradually convinced that they should receive holy communion often. The strict laws of eucharistic fasting from midnight contributed to this attitude, acting as a practical barrier that kept people from frequent communion. The ostensible purpose of these regulations was to encourage respect for the sacrament and to let people know that they should be well prepared to receive the Lord. Unfortunately, they also had this other effect of discouraging people from receiving frequently.

Given this background, and the importance people attach to the practices they have been taught as children, immediate acceptance of twentieth-century eucharistic reforms such as communion under both species and lay eucharistic ministry has to take time and experience. We must accept the fact that some people will feel ill at ease with the new options even if many have already accepted them.

II. Lay Ministry and the Eucharist

As with many changes, people wonder why something new has to be introduced into their lives. Our answer to the question, "why special ministers of the eucharist?" is simple: they are needed. This is what Pope Paul VI wanted the world to know when on January 29, 1973 he ordered to be promulgated a document known familiarly as *Immensae Caritatis* ("Immense Love") and more formally as, "Instruction on Facilitating Sacramental Communion in Particular Circumstances." This is a direct quote from it:

"Present-day conditions demand that . . . greater access to Holy Communion should be made possible so that the faithful, by sharing more fully in the fruits of the sacrifice of the Mass, might dedicate themselves more readily and effectively to God and to the good of the Church and of mankind. . . . First of all, provision must be made lest reception become impossible or difficult owing to a lack of a sufficient number of ministers."

This reflects the fact that in the whole history of the Church, ours is a unique era in which all these elements are simultaneously present: encouragement to the faithful to receive the Lord Jesus at every eucharist and under both species; the great numbers of lay people who do want to receive under at least one form; the relatively small numbers of ordinary ministers (priests and deacons) in relation to all members of a congregation.

When we go further back to seek the recent history of lay eucharistic ministry, and the significant sources for its flowering, we look to the documents of the Second Vatican Council, particularly the sections which emphasized the holiness of all the people of God, and the rights and duties which flow from their baptismal sacrament. We also notice the groundwork being laid for the needs we have today, that communion under both species was restored to the Church by the Constitution on the Sacred Liturgy (no. 55): "Communion under both kinds may be granted when the bishops think fit, not only to clerics and religious but also to the laity, in cases to be determined by the Apostolic See."

In 1969, the Missal of Pope Paul VI was published. This was the long-awaited reform of the Mass, and an extensive introduction, called the General Instruction, said this about ministries in the Mass (no. 58):

"In the community which assembles to celebrate Mass everyone has the right and duty to take an active part, though the ways in which individuals do so will differ according to the status and function of each. Each one, whether cleric or layman, should do all of, but only, those parts pertaining to his office, so that, from the very way in which the celebration is organized, the Church may be seen to consist of different orders and ministries."

A whole chapter is devoted to a description of the functions and ministries of those in sacred orders, of the functions and ministries of all God's people, and of special ministries at Mass. These initial writings have since been developed by ten years of practice. For instance, in November 1970 the American bishops, meeting in Washington, asked the Roman Congregation of the Sacraments to grant them the faculty to permit qualified lay persons to assist priests in giving holy communion. This was granted in March 1971 in cases where an ordinary minister was absent or hindered by age, bad health, or other demands of pastoral ministry, or when a very lengthy distribution of communion could not otherwise be avoided.

This special permission for the United States was granted for a one year period, and then it was renewed once. Evidently these two years were a time of testing and evaluation which contributed to proving the pastoral value of the practice, because on January 29, 1973, the instruction *Immensae Caritatis* extended to the universal church permission to implement the practice of lay people acting as ministers in the distribution of holy communion.

Immensae Caritatis provides us not just with a permission but also an ideal of how the pastoral needs of the people can be met. The following excerpts from the section of the document dealing with eucharistic ministers deserves careful reading.

"There are various circumstances in which a lack of sufficient ministers for the distribution of Holy Communion can occur:
—during Mass, because of the size of the congregation or a particular difficulty in which a celebrant finds himself;
—outside of Mass, when it is difficult because of distance to take the sacred species, especially the Viaticum, to the sick in danger of death, or when the very number of the sick, especially in hospitals and similar institutions, requires many ministers. Therefore, in order that the faithful, who are in the state of grace and who with an upright and pious disposition, wish to share in the Sacred Banquet, may not be deprived of this sacramental help and consolation, it has seemed appropriate to the Holy Father to establish extraordinary ministers,

["extraordinary" was the official translation in documents prior to 1978 when the word "special" was introduced as being more suitable], who may give Holy Communion to themselves and to other faithful under the following determined conditions:

I. Local Ordinaries have the faculty to permit a suitable person individually chosen as an extraordinary minister for a specific occasion or for a time or, in the case of necessity, in some permanent way, either to give the Eucharist to himself or to other faithful and to take it to the sick who are confined to their homes. This faculty may be used whenever
a) there is no priest, deacon or acolyte;
b) these are prevented from administering Holy Communion because of another pastoral ministry or because of ill health or advanced age;
c) the number of faithful requesting Holy Communion is such that the celebration of Mass or the distribution of the Eucharist outside of Mass would be unduly prolonged.

II. Local Ordinaries also have the faculty to permit individual priests exercising their sacred office to appoint a suitable person who in cases of genuine necessity would distribute Holy Communion for a specific occasion.

VI. If time permits, it is fitting that the suitable person individually chosen by the Local Ordinary for administering Holy Communion, as well as the person appointed by a priest having the faculty spoken of in number II, should receive the mandate according to the rite annexed to this Instruction; they are to distribute Holy Communion according to the liturgical norms.

Since these faculties are granted only for the spiritual good of the faithful and for cases of genuine necessity, priests are to remember that they are not thereby excused from the task of distributing the Eucharist to the faithful who legitimately request it, and especially from taking and giving it to the sick."

We can deduce from a reading of this document that there is an underlying acceptance of certain ideas: that all baptized Catholics have the right to receive in their own hands and under both species, and that not only the clergy but also other members of the Church can be trusted to carry the eucharist to the sick.

A further foundational assumption of this instruction is the ecclesiology expressed in no. 10 of the Vatican II document on The Church, that the common priesthood of the faithful and the ministerial or hierarchical priesthood both share in the one priesthood of Christ, and so all baptized people have parts to play in the sanctification of the world, and all are holy and pleasing to God.

And finally, in appreciating what led up to *Immensae Caritatis*, we realize that in addition to the historical rightness of lay eucharistic ministry, and without lessening respect for the eucharist, Pope Paul felt a pressing responsibility to make the sacrament of the Lord's Body and Blood as accessible as possible to all who can benefit by receiving it.

Acceptance of the spirit and permissions of *Immensae Caritatis* was not immediate. People remain faithful to the attitudes they grow up with, and have to be drawn away from them to

new approaches by exposure to the facts of history and to the pastoral advantages of the new permissions initiated by our spiritual leaders, the pope and the bishops.

TYPES OF EUCHARISTIC MINISTRY

There are two major similar yet distinct types of special eucharistic ministry: ministers at the eucharist and ministers to the sick. Some people assist in the distribution of holy communion at Mass, as either ministers of the bread or ministers of the cup. Some people carry holy communion to the sick at home or in a hospital or nursing facility. In some parishes, people are asked to perform just one of these services; in other situations, one person might undertake each of the eucharistic ministries at different times.

It is true that the person who assists at Mass is a liturgical minister; but in fact so is the person who carries the eucharist to someone else, for this is not a mere job of transportation, but rather an extension of the parish's liturgy. The ministers to the sick should always try to "bring Church" to the people they visit, by having a prepared program of liturgical activity, tailored, of course, to the comfort and attention span of the people involved. In its fullest form, there will be greetings, a penitential rite, readings from Scripture, reflections upon the Word, the Lord's Prayer, giving of holy communion, and a concluding rite. (See Appendix II for a model of this kind of communion service.)

SELECTION OF MINISTERS

The prudent selection of respected persons to undertake this ministry will help assure a parish community's acceptance of special eucharistic ministers. Given human nature, in this as in other matters, people form their opinions about a new practice based upon, first, their opinion of the people who do it, and second, the performance of the people who do it.

Having offered this as a necessary caution for those responsible for choosing eucharistic ministers, we must also beware of narrow or prejudicial attitudes in seeking volunteers or selecting applicants. For instance, while the pastors of a parish will typically be the ones responsible for the final choice of ministers, they would do well to solicit the suggestions of other parish leaders for the names of people they feel would command the respect of the congregation.

Everyone in the parish should know that *Immensae Caritatis* excludes neither men nor women from this ministry, and sets no age limit at all. People should have a chance to ponder the descriptive words (given below) of the Roman instruction about the "suitable person" to be chosen, and should be aware of any local diocesan policies on the subject. For example, some American dioceses may establish a minimum age for this ministry (which might reasonably be waived in a school setting). It may even be that the bishop who leads the diocese does not want to make use of the papal permission at all, and chooses not to have any special eucharistic ministers functioning in his diocese. But where permission from the bishop has been given, both men and women (including children and the elderly) are eligible to serve, and should be invited to do so, so that the baptismal dignity and royal priesthood of the faithful of every segment of the parish will be clearly asserted and manifested.

Immensae Caritatis gives us a general picture of the kind of person who is to be called to this ministry:

"The person who has been appointed to be an extraordinary minister of Holy Communion is necessarily to be duly instructed and should distinguish himself by his [her] Christian life, faith, and morals. Let him [her] strive to be worthy of this great office; let him [her] cultivate devotion to the Holy Eucharist and show himself [herself] as an example to the other faithful by his [her] piety and reverence for this most holy Sacrament of the altar. Let no one be chosen whose selection may cause scandal among the faithful."

On a first reading, many good people who are modest about their own spirituality and who have a healthy awareness of their own sinfulness might be discouraged by this paragraph and think that they are simply unworthy to hold this office.

That is not why the paragraph was written. Certainly for individuals to be considered, their pastoral leaders must already have confidence in the Christian quality of their lives. The true impact of the description is that each minister is urged to grow in love for the eucharist, to personify even more deeply the love of Christ for others, and to be sensitive to the high moral standards that we always want to see in each other, but especially in those chosen for special service.

Pastors will have a special responsibility to continue to provide direction and resources for their eucharistic ministers. Opportunities for discussions, suggestions, shared prayer will be beneficial. Area conferences or Vicariates should sponsor days of recollection or retreats. Reading material and alternative prayers can stimulate new ideas and appreciation about the mystery and power of the eucharistic sacrament.

People who take part in liturgical events are usually changed by them. The minister's faith and prayer will most likely be affected by the holiness of the people that he or she comes into contact with, and by the marvelous proximity of the One who is given to others. Just as a conscientious and sincere doctor will become a better doctor after some experience and reflection, so too a special eucharistic minister can expect to become more sensitive to and appreciative of God's graciousness, mankind's dignity, and the marvelous power of the eucharistic sacrament, through the performance of this ministry.

MINISTRY, EUCHARIST, LITURGY
It should be clear that the faith of a eucharistic minister is very important. Each one must believe what the Church believes, that when we receive holy communion, we take into our bodies the Body and Blood—the Person—of Jesus Christ. The eucharist is not food that represents Christ, or food to make us remember him. It is Christ. It is the risen Lord who at his final Passover meal gave this gift to be continually shared out among those who have faith in him.

The Church has several names for this gift. The most familiar is *holy communion*. Holy, because it is specially related to God, and communion, meaning to be one with. When we receive holy communion, we are one with God, and we share unity with other people who also receive this sacrament.

19

The word *eucharist* means thanksgiving, or praise. It is a proper title for both the liturgy of the Mass and for the Body and Blood of the Lord that is consecrated within the Mass.

When the sacrament is reserved, that is, kept in a safe place for personal devotion and to take to the sick, it is termed the *Blessed Sacrament*: blessed, or helpful for salvation, and sacrament—an outward, visible sign of an invisible reality.

The Passover meal aspect of the eucharist has been thoroughly researched and restored to prominence in the last decades. We begin the Mass with the equivalent of a synagogue service—a liturgy of the word in which we listen to the Law and the prophets and now in the new era, the Gospel; we respond to these divine messages with psalms and hymns, and we make present-day applications of the eternal word to our lives. Then, having heard about God's love, we respond with a prayer of thanksgiving—a liturgy of the eucharist which climaxes in the reception of holy communion.

This is prompted by the Passover practice of Jesus at the Last Supper, when he said blessings over the bread and wine, praising his Father as all pious Jews were accustomed to do. He then made this paschal meal his own by the mysterious and awesome additions: this is my body; this is my blood, before passing the bread and wine out for his friends to consume.

We follow that pattern in the liturgy of the eucharist. We praise and thank God; the priest, standing in the place of the Lord, takes the bread and wine and blesses them and gives them out, no longer bread and wine, but holy communion.

Their outward form and appearance stay the same. They still taste like, smell like, look like bread and wine, but in this case we trust in our faith and do not rely on our senses to tell us the truth. Our confidence is in Christ and all he said and did, and so when the priest or minister of the eucharist invites us to receive Jesus with the words "The body of Christ," "The blood of Christ" we show that we believe that Christ is really present in the eucharistic species by saying, "Amen."

III. Ministerial Procedures at Mass

While we have all been to Mass many times, most of us have never thought about it as a *liturgy*. Literally, the word "liturgy" means "work of the people." A liturgy is a public activity of a community for the benefit of its people and their goals.

When we use the word "liturgy," we are specifically referring to the public worship that the Church offers to God—communion services, the liturgy of the hours, the celebration of the sacraments, but above all, the celebration of the Mass. And we rejoice in the fact that our liturgies are never just human activity. They do not depend for their power or their effectiveness solely on human initiative. The celebration of our sacred liturgy is always the work of the whole Church, Christ himself as the Head, and we as the members of his Body.

At the liturgy of the Mass, we have a presiding celebrant, perhaps with concelebrants and deacons assisting; we have other ministers of the liturgy such as lectors, cantors, ushers, musicians, choir members, servers, special ministers of the eucharist; and we have front row people, middle-of-the-church people, and back wall people. Each one is a participant with the potential to add or detract from the celebration; but realistically, it is the celebrant and the other ministers who carry the greatest burden for the skillful and reverent accomplishment of the service.

All ministers must be aware of this. They are called to make a contribution to the liturgy that is positive and effective. The members of the congregation form an impression about the ministers which affects their feelings about being at Mass that day. The attitude, the appearance, and the performance of a minister all matter to the other participants at a liturgy. Not only is this true at Mass, but it also applies to the minister to the sick who is the celebrant of that communion service and has the responsibility to make that liturgy as prayerful and satisfying as possible.

THE MINISTER AT MASS

We will now briefly describe some practical procedures that special eucharistic ministers can follow at the liturgy of the Mass. Naturally, there are many variables that will affect this model, such as the size of the sanctuary, the decision whether to give holy communion under both species or only under the form of bread, the numbers of communicants and the numbers of ministers. While we would all like to be perfect from the start, and never have to readjust things later, it really is a good idea to experiment and evaluate before establishing a definitive routine.

Before Mass begins, the special eucharistic ministers meet the celebrant in the sacristy or perhaps in the back of the church, and should process with him into the church to the sanctuary. The ministers walk in procession behind the servers and the lector and in front of the deacon and priest. Regular clothing of a dignified appearance is to be worn. No albs or other liturgical vesture are required.

After a genuflection to the Blessed Sacrament or reverent bow to the altar, the ministers take their reserved seats, either in the sanctuary or very close to it. This ceremonial entrance should be the norm for Sundays and major celebrations. On weekdays or in informal groups the ministers could simply sit in the congregation if they so desire, provided that they can reach the altar without delay while the sign of peace is exchanged.

The ministers have no particular responsibility until after the sign of peace. Before the "Lamb of God" chant is said or sung, the ministers should approach the altar and group themselves near it. If loaves of bread have to be broken, or flagons of wine poured into cups, the special ministers should assist with reverence and unrushed dignity, once the celebrant or deacon has begun the ritual action of breaking and pouring. If some ministers are not needed to help, they simply stand in place and participate in the singing, which is not limited to only three invocations of the "Lamb of God, you take away the sins of the world . . .," but should continue until the sacred species have been prepared for distribution. We are not in a hurry at this time, and no one should act in haste. This is a great tradition: the "Lamb of God" chant was introduced into the Mass specifically as a beautiful complement to the ritual action of breaking the bread and pouring the wine and preparing them for distribution.

If communion is to be given only under the form of bread, and waferlike hosts are used, the ministers of course would not have any of this to do, but would simply stand near the altar in readiness to serve.

While "It is most desirable that people should receive the body of the Lord in hosts consecrated at the same Mass" (General Instruction on the Mass, no. 56h), it will sometimes be necessary to distribute hosts already consecrated and reserved in the tabernacle. If this is the case, a deacon or special minister should go to the tabernacle at the time of the Lamb of God chant and bring to the altar the required number of ciboria. (Ciboria are the airtight vessels that hold the eucharistic bread. [The singular is ciborium]. The bread, or hosts, may also be on a paten, which is like a dish or plate. Chalices, or cups, hold the eucharistic wine.)

Whether the special ministers should stand or kneel when the celebrant elevates the Body of Christ ("This is the Lamb of God. . .") can be decided within the parish. Both postures are reverent. If the congregation customarily kneels at that point, the ministers might feel more comfortable doing the same. Alternatively, the ministers might remain standing and be ready to begin their service. It might also be easier and more practical for some arthritic or elderly ministers not to have to kneel, since they might not be able to rise without the nearby support of chair or pew.

As the celebrant receives the bread and drinks from the cup, the ministers should stand if they are not doing so already, and should step closer to the altar. The celebrant will give each minister communion, first the body of the Lord, and then the precious blood. The original instruction for special ministers allowed them to self-communicate the bread and

drink from the cup, without receiving them from the celebrant. Since then, this procedure has been restudied, and it
is now clearly stated that the celebrant or the deacon should
give the bread and then the cup to each special minister. Even
if this takes a little more time, it has the value of demonstrat-
ing that our liturgy is hierarchical, that we share one bread
and one cup, and that even for the special ministers, a
cafeteria self-serve style is not appropriate.

After the special ministers have received from the chalice
(and this is the privilege of the assisting ministers even if the
congregation is not receiving under both species), they take
their chalice, ciborium or bread plate from the priest, or from
the altar, and go to their communion stations. Each minister
of the cup picks up a purificator, the white cleansing cloth
used to wipe the lip of the chalice.

Each parish has to work out the best arrangement for communion stations, particularly when communion under both
species is being given. Older churches with a narrow space
between the sanctuary and the pews present difficult traffic
flow problems. For those who choose not to drink from the
cup, room must be left so that they can pass by easily. A
practical rule-of-thumb is that there should be two ministers
of the cup for each minister of the bread. If necessary, the
ministers of the cup can stand together, but it would be better
to have one on each side of each minister of the bread.

As the communicant approaches, the minister of the bread
should slightly elevate the host or the bread and say, "The
Body of Christ." The communicant will answer, "Amen,"
and then the minister places the eucharist in the hollow of the
person's hand, or on his tongue.

The minister of the cup similarly addresses the communicant,
saying, "The Blood of Christ." After the "Amen," he hands
the cup to the person and lets the other person hold it and
drink from it. When the cup is handed back, the minister
wipes the lip of the cup with the purificator. The minister
then turns the cup slightly before repeating the process with
the next communicant.

A minister may wonder, or be asked by a friend, if this practice of drinking from the same cup is dangerous to health. A spokesman for the American Medical Association was asked for an opinion, and gave this reassuring answer: "As far as we know, there is no scientific evidence of the transmission of disease to communicants using a common cup. The alcoholic content of the wine plus the hygenic practice of wiping the cup and turning it to a new position for each communicant seems to remove any danger."

Unfortunately, some people will remain unconvinced of this, and will never feel comfortable receiving from the cup. Whenever someone has a heavy cold or sickness, it would be only sensible for that person to refrain from drinking from the cup. Even in these exceptional cases, people are never to be permitted to take the bread and then dip it into the chalice themselves. There is too much danger of the dripping of the precious blood.

There is another way of giving holy communion under both species, and this is called intinction. The priest or minister takes a host (something more breadlike is not very practical) and dips it in the precious blood and places it on the person's tongue. While this is permitted, it is not the full sign of eucharistic sharing that taking the bread and drinking from the cup is. Also, intinction eliminates the possibility of a person receiving in the hand. However, on occasion, a parish may decide to give communion in this way, and eucharistic ministers should be aware of the proper procedure in such cases: perhaps with an assistant to hold the ciborium, the minister would hold the chalice, take a host and dip it into the blood, and (being careful to avoid drippings onto the floor) say, "The Body and Blood of Christ," wait for the "Amen," and then place the eucharist on the person's tongue.

When the last person has come up for communion, the celebrant should place his ciborium or paten on the altar and return to his chair. He should not be the one to cleanse the vessels or clear the altar. Deacons, eucharistic ministers, and servers should take responsibility for these actions. Not only does this manifest the hierarchy of ministries at liturgy, but it also allows the celebrant to have some time for personal prayer after communion, without unduly delaying the Mass.

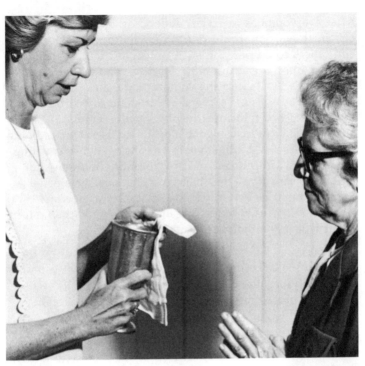

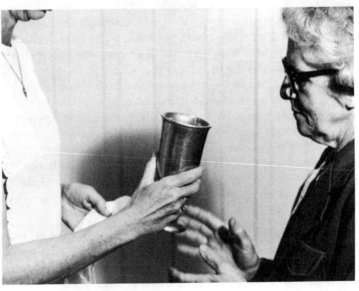

After everyone has received, depending upon the number of ministers, some could return directly to their places, and others could perform such functions as: 1)collecting the remaining bread into one ciborium, and taking it to the tabernacle; 2) cleansing communion plates (if they have been used by assisting servers) by brushing any particles into the chalices, and returning the plates to the servers; 3) taking all of the chalices to a side table or the sacristy; 4) consuming the precious blood immediately and discreetly, or covering the chalices with purificators and returning to them after Mass; 5) cleansing all the chalices and ciboria at a side table, or what might be better, leaving them on the side table and cleansing them after Mass. The ministers should then return to their places without delay.

The special ministers should have taken their seats by the time that the celebrant is ready to begin the prayer after communion. At the dismissal, they regroup and leave the church in procession with the celebrant, deacon, lectors, servers, etc.

After the Mass has ended—and only if necessary, while Mass is being concluded—the special ministers should go to the sacristy to take care of the sacred vessels. In the sacristy, they should first consume any of the precious blood remaining in the chalices. Then they should put some water in each chalice and ciborium, and brush any particles from the patens that have been used by the priest into the water. The water in each vessel should be swirled around to cleanse the whole inside, and then that water should either be consumed or poured into the sacrarium. This is the auxiliary sink found in each sacristy, which leads to a small dry well in the ground near the wall of the church. Then water should be used again to thoroughly wash and rinse all the vessels, especially those parts from which people have been drinking. Soap is not necessary nor ordinarily used, but when it is, be sure to rinse it all off.

For all of this washing and final drying, which really takes only a moment, the purificators can be used, if they are clean, or other cloths, called ablution cloths. All the vessels should be dried and returned to their usual storage place.

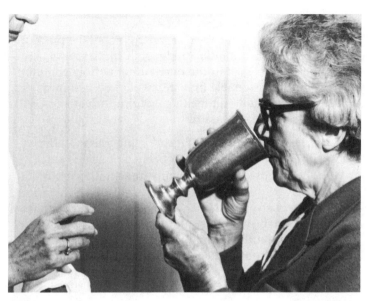

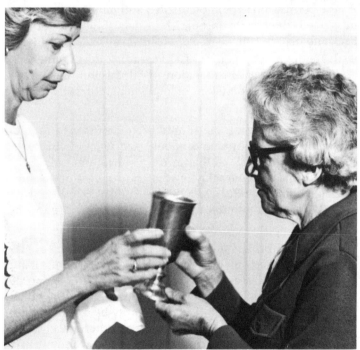

If the priests of a parish have reservations about the practicality of giving holy communion under both species, or of allowing lay people to assist in the distribution of holy communion, or both, a reasonable first step would be to initiate the procedures for a limited time (e.g., during Advent or Lent) and only at weekday Masses.

This approach has the advantage of being a limited experiment with a well-known and probably very stable small group. There should be no difficulty in getting ministers, although the very piety of the people might cause them to discount themselves at first, and so a personal invitation from the priest might be necessary. And if there are fears of showing favoritism, let the first announcement be an open one, inviting anyone to volunteer, but with a notice that the bishop requires the priests to suggest candidates based on suitability as well as desire.

As the permissions are implemented and ministers are commissioned, the priests and parish leaders should seek feedback and observe the degree of acceptance. They should also evaluate the practical questions of coordination of ministers, and time and space considerations. With this information and experience, further decisions of implementation will be easier to make.

While only worthy people should be commissioned as special ministers, their numbers should not be too restricted. This is both practical, as the need for substitutes will arise, and theological, as we acknowledge the holiness of the general membership of the Church. The August 1976 *Newsletter* of the Bishops' Committee on the Liturgy made the following suggestion:

"As a general principle it is by far preferable to increase the number of eucharistic ministers than to have a minister function at several Masses on any particular day. The extraordinary minister should fulfill his/her role at the Mass in which he/she participates and should not simply be assigned and waiting (in the sacristy, rectory, or some other place) to distribute communion at several celebrations. Certainly in any given parish a sufficient number of qualified persons can be found to function as extraordinary ministers at the Sunday Masses which they attend and thus render it unnecessary for any extraordinary ministers to assist at more than one Mass. Here is a case where a too strict limitation of the number of special ministers would frustrate the proper development of this liturgical ministry."

As was indicated earlier, a eucharistic minister has a unique and specific function to perform at liturgy, and should not "double up," acting as a lector, usher, or leader of song at one and the same Mass. It is understandable that this might have to be done in an emergency, but to respect the variety and integrity of all ministries, this should never be planned.

Consistent with the Church's desire to give experience in ministry to as many people as possible, and the conviction that many people are truly gifted for these ministries, it would seem to be a wise policy to commission ministers only for a limited period of time (e.g., three years) after which they not actively serve as eucharistic ministers, but are given a reprieve from liturgical responsibility, or invited to take on some other ministry, e.g., lector or usher.

This is beneficial and liberating, perhaps to the former minister, who might appreciate a change, and certainly to the new minister who will have the opportunity to serve in his place. (The exception to this might be made in favor of the minister to a sick person who has built up a personal rapport and relationship that would be hard for the sick person to give up.) And it is for the common good of the parish to have the experience of responsibility for our public worship shared by as many parishioners as possible.

If this term-of-office policy is mentioned in advance as a condition of service, and the reasons for rotation explained, it probably will be well accepted, and could lead to a rejuvenation of other ministries. If there are eucharistic ministers presently functioning who were commissioned without any mention of a term of office, justice and tact suggest that the new policy be explained but not rigorously applied to them. Hopefully, if this is parish policy, they will want to abide by

31

it. And it could well be agreed that after a certain amount of time has elapsed, individuals could be restored to eucharistic ministry for another term.

DISTRIBUTION OF ASHES

An exception to the rule of not performing two ministries at one Mass might be necessary on Ash Wednesday, when extraordinary crowds coming to church can interfere with the flow of the Mass. During the Masses of this day, the distribution of ashes should take place after the homily within the liturgy of the word. Because too few clergy may be present to accomplish this distribution in a reasonable time, special ministers of the eucharist can help. In the January 1980 *Newsletter* of the U.S. Bishops' Committee on the Liturgy, we read:

"According to a response from the Congregation for Divine Worship (January 1975) other persons may be associated with the bishop or priest in the imposition of ashes, e.g., deacons, special ministers of communion and other lay persons, when there is a true pastoral need. Special ministers of communion and deacons may bring blessed ashes to the sick and those confined to their homes. If a minister is not available, a member of the family or another person may bring blessed ashes to a shut-in, using one of the formularies in the Sacramentary to impose the ashes."

Special ministers should know before Mass that they will be called upon to distribute ashes. After the homily, those who will help with the distribution of ashes should come forward. The priest will impose ashes on the forehead of each minister saying either, "Remember you are dust and to dust you shall return," or "Turn away from your sins and believe in the good news." The priest will hand each minister a vessel with ashes and he or she will go to a station. As people approach to receive ashes, the minister places the thumb in the bowl and traces the sign of the cross on each person's forehead with the thumb, saying the same words the priest says. Afterwards, the ministers can take the vessels back to the sacristy and wash their hands. Then they return unobtrusively to their seats.

Another assistance that non-ordained members of the congregation can provide for their clergy and congregants is to help in the blessing of throats on the feast of St. Blaise (February 3).

While permission for people other than clergy to pray this blessing has been granted for the universal Church, whether it is done in your parish depends upon a) whether your diocesan bishop has decided to use the permission, and b) whether the local pastor feels the need for assistance.

On November 10, 1985, our Bishops' Committee on the Liturgy published a *Rite of Blessing of Throats* which was an excerpt of the forthcoming *Book of Blessings.* A key section stated that the blessing of throats may be given by a priest, a deacon, or with the permission of the bishop, by a properly designated lay minister.

Traditionally, the blessing is given by touching the throat of each person with two candles which were blessed on the Feast of the Presentation (February 2). The candles should be joined in the form of a cross, and either of two forms for the blessing are provided:

Through the intercession of St. Blaise, bishop and martyr, may God deliver you from every disease of the throat and from every other illness: in the name of the Father, and of the Son, ✠ and of the Holy Spirit. Amen.
Or:
(Name), may God preserve you by the prayers of St. Blaise from sore throats and all illness, through Christ our Lord. Amen.

While the ordinary practice is to give the blessing after the Liturgy of the Word at a Mass, the blessing can also be done after a Liturgy of the Word outside of Mass. It is permitted for the blessing to be given to the sick or elderly in their homes when they cannot attend the parish celebration. Thus there is clear advantage in having Special Ministers—lay persons who are already approved by the bishop and known to the congregation—as helpers of the celebrant at crowded Masses and/or as ministers of charity to the sick when the clergy cannot visit them on St. Blaise's Day.

IV. Communion to the Sick

Not only is it allowed but also recommended that holy communion be carried from the Sunday eucharist of the community to those who are unable to be at the eucharist. A rite for bringing holy communion to people outside of Mass was published in Rome in June 1973 and no. 14 of the introduction says this:

"In fact it is proper that those who are prevented from being present at the community's celebration should be refreshed with the eucharist. In this way they may realize that they are united not only with the Lord's sacrifice but also with the community itself and are supported by the love of their brothers and sisters."

The introduction goes on to say that pastors should provide this opportunity to the sick and aged "frequently, and if pos-

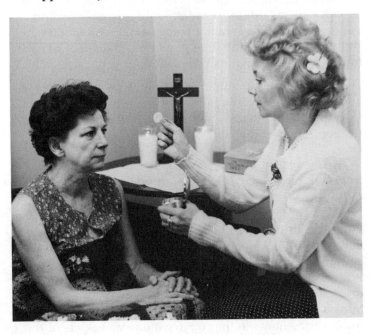

sible, daily, especially during the Easter season." While parish priests have traditionally been very sensitive to this hunger for the eucharist on the part of the sick and aged, bringing communion to the homebound on Sunday has not been generally feasible. Now, with the willing assistance of special eucharistic ministers, it can be done, and should be done.

Special training, even beyond that given to the ministers at Mass, should be provided for the ministers to the sick. Notice must be taken of the particular circumstance of the communicant. A minister might carry the eucharist to one person alone in an apartment, or to a bedridden person with relatives present, or to a group of sick people in a nursing home or hospital ward. Especially in the last case, a professional familiar with the attitudes and emotions of the sick and elderly should provide some advice and practical hints about how to approach them (e.g., speak loudly, greet everyone, don't be upset by interruptions) and how to cope with emergencies and hospital protocol (what to do if the person is indisposed; what requests should you politely ignore.) Basically, any sensible, considerate person who loves people and is bringing them the Lord of their lives cannot miss succeeding in this ministry. Each minister should ideally have only one or perhaps two calls, so that he or she could spend time with each sick person.

Special ministers should not be surprised if some people, especially the elderly, remembering the older eucharistic traditions, may wish to settle just for having a priest bring them holy communion once a month. Gently but persuasively, this new service should be explained and continually be offered to the sick. A eucharistic minister could accompany the priest on the First Friday call, and it should be made clear that the special ministry on Sunday is in addition to and does not replace the priest's visits. It is entirely acceptable if the potential recipient wishes to refuse the offer. It simply is a good thing to make an extra effort to offer this service to members of the parish.

The special ministers to the sick have permission to take the eucharist to the homebound or hospitalized at any suitable time, but there is a special significance to carrying the eucharist directly from Mass to the communicant. There are two possible models to follow for this.

One procedure is for the minister to stay until the end of the Mass, greet his neighbors, wait for the church to empty, and then go to the tabernacle, take the eucharist and place it in the small, secure container, called a pyx, and then leave the church and proceed to the waiting communicant.

The other possibility is for the celebrant, after distributing holy communion to the congregation, to take a pyx, and place in it the amount of consecrated bread that a special minister will need. The pyx, or pyxes, are placed on the altar; everything else is cleared away. The special ministers remain in their seats until after the communion prayer, and then the celebrant may call them to the altar and address them in this or a similar way:

"My dear friends, you are now to carry the Body of our Lord from this eucharistic assembly to our brothers and sisters who are unable to be here with us. Give them our greetings and our love, read today's Holy Scriptures with them, pray with them, and minister to them this most precious sacrament."

Then the special ministers are handed the pyxes by the priest. They place them in their coat or shirt pockets or purses. They then go to the foot of the altar for the recessional, and the celebrant bestows the final blessing and gives the dismissal. The special ministers process out with the celebrant, and proceed immediately to their destinations. On the way, they can talk with other people, but long or multiple conversations would not be seemly and should be avoided during the performance of this ministry. The exception would be if other people share a car ride or similar shared space.

If when the minister arrives in the home, more people wish to receive than the minister was expecting, he could break the bread into several parts. Conversely, if he has bread remain-

ing, he can either consume the remaining bread or return it to the tabernacle.

If the communicant should drop the host to the floor, or even spit it out, the minister should calmly pick it up, place it in a handkerchief or cloth, and eventually put it in the small water bowl near the tabernacle and put the bowl into the tabernacle. The bread will dissolve and the contents of the bowl can be emptied into the sacrarium.

If someone is unable to take any solid food, and is thus unable to receive even a small piece of the bread, it is lawful to minister holy communion under the form of wine to that person. The minister would need to place some of the precious blood in a sealed container and carry it to the sick person that way. Ordinarily, only the consecrated bread would be carried to the sick.

The 1973 instruction on holy communion outside of Mass speaks of wearing liturgical vesture that is traditional or appropriate. In our circumstance, ordinary dignified street clothing is what the minister should wear. The people of the parish should be informed that when holy communion is to be brought to a private or nursing home for a sick or aged person, a suitable table should be prepared in the room with a clean cloth covering, and possibly a crucifix. Candles also should be provided. These small but valuable efforts prepare for the entrance of the Lord into one's environment. Some people also like to be able to take a drink of water after receiving, and this too should be made ready. A friendly greeting when the minister arrives is not disrespectful to the Lord. The pyx is placed on the table, and the candles should be lit if this has not been done already. The minister could chat for awhile, or proceed directly with the service, leave time for meditative prayer after the person has received, and have coffee or tea afterwards if it is offered. Make the person aware of what is happening in the parish; always bring a bulletin. Realize that the Lord chooses to be present in you as well as in the sacrament. (For a more complete model of a communion service to the sick, see Appendix II.)

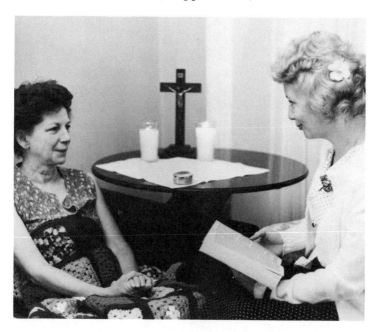

Pyxes, like chalices and ciboria, no longer have to be made of precious metal. As long as they are secure, solid, and dignified, they are adequate; of course, their beauty will also be admired. If the parish purchases enough small pyxes, the ministers could simply take them home afterwards and bring them to Mass the following week. Otherwise, they might have to return them to the sacristy that same day.

In this facet of special eucharistic ministry, just as at the Mass, there should be more than enough trained and commissioned ministers to provide this service without allowing it to become a burden for particular individuals. Not everyone can give weekly service, and sometimes people can be very demanding; therefore, the director of this ministry should promise only what is reasonable, stay alert to needed changes in schedules and relationships, and help people get replacements when needed.

V. Commissioning for Single Occasions

Given the public nature and significance of special eucharistic ministry, there are several preliminary requirements that all candidates for eucharistic ministry ordinarily will fulfill: invitation from or acceptance by the parish clergy; hours of discussion and teaching about the theology of the eucharist, both as sacrament and liturgical celebration; preparation for both the usual and exceptional situations; opportunities for practice and critique; and a formal commissioning ceremony by the bishop himself or one of his delegates. (For guidance and personal reflection, the official Rite of Commissioning Special Ministers of Holy Communion is included in Appendix I of this book.)

However, the situation may arise that the expected ministers, ordinary or special, are not available to assist at Mass, and there are no commissioned special ministers present, and there is a very large number of people who wish to receive.

In this situation of genuine necessity, *Immensae Caritatis* provides a solution for the pastoral benefit of the people, so that the Mass is not unduly delayed or some people under pressure of time leave the church without receiving. The bishop of the diocese has the faculty to give his priests the permission "to appoint a suitable person who in cases of genuine necessity would distribute Holy Communion for a specific occasion."

The way that this would be done is specified in a separate chapter of the Rite of Commissioning Special Ministers: "During the breaking of the bread and the commingling, the person who is to distribute holy communion comes to the altar and stands before the celebrant. After the *Lamb of God* the priest blesses him/her with these words:

**Today you are to distribute
the body and blood of Christ
to your brothers and sisters.
May the Lord bless ✠ you, N.**

℟. **Amen.**

When the priest has himself received holy communion in the usual way, he gives communion to the minister of the eucharist. Then he gives him/her the paten, or other vessels with the hosts. Then they go to give communion to the people."

Consistent with this flexibility in the light of particular needs and circumstances is the permission that has been granted for a person who is not already a minister to carry the eucharist to someone sick at home. The June–July 1978 issue of the Bishops' Committee on the Liturgy *Newsletter* gave an affirmative answer to the question whether a person could be commissioned on a single occasion to carry the eucharist after Sunday Mass to a member of his family who is sick.

The section of *Immensae Caritatis* about priests having the permission to appoint a suitable person on a specific occasion in cases of genuine need was then quoted in support of the answer, which thus implied a broadening of "genuine need" in this aspect of the ministry to include situations of genuine good for the family concerned. Certainly, if a regular churchgoer is temporarily incapacitated, and there is no time to provide a formal commissioning (there should always have been some time for instruction during the adult education program within the parish), and no one would be as suitable to bring holy communion to this person as a spouse or grown child, it can be done by that member of the family. The spiritual and social benefits can be tremendous. This is not to downplay the value and effectiveness of special ministers who are not members of the family, nor to say that every situation will be best served by a member of the family performing this function, but we should consider this possibility.

If the decision is made to have an individual who is not already a special minister carry the eucharist to the sick person, he or she should be given a special blessing similar to the one given above for ad hoc ministers at Mass. Depending on the practice of the parish, it might be given publicly when the other ministers to the sick depart, or privately after Mass is over. The Rite does not provide a distinct prayer for this, and so the priest could pray as he sees fit, or he could use this formula:

**Today you are to bring
the body of Christ
to your brother (sister) N. who is ill.
May this spiritual food strengthen him/her
and may the Lord bless ✠ you, N.
as you perform this ministry.**

The same issue (June–July 1978) of the BCL *Newsletter* dealt with the question of oversupply of ministers: should special ministers of the eucharist assist in the distribution of holy communion if priests and deacons are available, e.g., at a concelebration. The reply is simple and directly from *Immensae Caritatis*: special ministers should function only when there is a genuine pastoral need. If there is a sufficient number of priests and deacons to give holy communion, special ministers are not needed. It is incongruous and incorrect to have ordinary ministers of the eucharist return to their seats while special ministers distribute the eucharist.

The one exception to this rule or the time when it could be waived, would be at the Mass for the Commissioning of Special Ministers. At that Mass, some of the newly commissioned ministers might exercise their ministry.

In the following chapter, five practical questions which may be put to a special minister of the eucharist will be addressed.

VI. Questions Frequently Asked

How long does a person have to fast before receiving Holy Communion?

People in good health are obliged to fast from food and alcoholic drink for one hour prior to receiving holy communion.

People who are sick can take medicine and non-alcoholic drinks at any time before receiving holy communion. This concession was first granted by Pope Pius XII, and continues in force.

There is a value in some fast for those who are able, out of respect for the special character of the eucharistic food they are going to receive. Part 3 of *Immensae Caritatis* speaks of "a time of silence and recollection before the reception of Holy Communion. In the case of the sick, however, it will be a sufficient sign of piety and reverence if, for a brief period, they turn their minds to the greatness of the mystery."

The Instruction goes on to give new norms for the period of time for the sick to abstain from food and alcoholic drink: approximately one quarter of an hour, for those who are sick at home or in a hospital, for the aged who must remain at home, for sick and elderly priests who wish to say Mass or receive holy communion, and for "persons looking after the sick and the aged wishing to receive Holy Communion with them, whenever they are unable to observe the fast of one hour without inconvenience."

This kind of fasting, whether fifteen minutes or one hour, is intended to be a period of spiritual preparation for the eucharist. Water does not break the fast and can be taken at any time by anyone before receiving.

Can a person receive twice on the same day?

In general, Catholics can receive holy communion more than once in a day, if they are participating in distinctly different eucharistic celebrations. For example, if a person goes to a regular weekday Mass and receives holy communion, and later learns that the funeral Mass immediately afterwards is for a friend, that person could stay and receive holy communion again. Similarly, if one attends a Sunday Mass, and then in the afternoon goes to a wedding Mass, he or she could receive again. A person should not receive holy communion at each Mass if he or she is staying in church for the 7 and the 8 and the 9 o'clock Masses.

The question may arise whether a eucharistic minister, present on the altar and assisting at more than one Mass on a particular day, should receive at each Mass. Something may be said both pro and con on this question: positively, that sharing in holy communion is the fullest sharing in the celebration, and a minister of the Mass should naturally be receiving (which is one of the criticisms of the "fireman" approach of a priest appearing from the sacristy just to help with holy communion, without participating in the whole Mass); negatively, that this could become an abuse too, and the people could wonder why this was being allowed to others but not to them.

The best answer lies in moderation. There should be enough eucharistic ministers so that multiple assignments on a single day are extremely infrequent. In such infrequent cases, receiving again would seem to be acceptable.

If a special minister takes holy communion to someone who is sick at home, can he or she give holy communion to other Catholics in the house?

This will depend on the circumstances. A special minister is a steward, or custodian, of the sacrament; he or she has the obligation to be very careful about sharing the sacrament. For example, it would be perfectly correct to bring holy communion to other members of the household who are unable to get to church that day, as long as they express a desire for it and are members of the Catholic Church in the state of grace. But this should not be presumed, both for the sake of propriety and to prevent guilt feelings on the part of someone who would have liked to go to confession first, for example.

Also, one cannot presume that everyone values the eucharist in the same way; some good people will think that it is a "nice thing" to receive, merely out of plain politeness. This is not an adequate reason for receiving. Another possibility is that the minister may meet non-church-going Catholics who could and should be attending Mass at church. Clearly, unless they are unable to go to church because of the constant care to the sick person the minister would not give holy communion to them. If the other members of the family will receive at Mass that day, they would not be given communion at this time. As a guideline, if you enter a home and meet someone there in addition to the person you were sent to, you could inquire if they want to receive. If they do, discuss it a little bit. Remind them that sacramental confession must precede a worthy reception of holy communion if there is serious sin that needs to be reconciled. In the long run, that kind of frank discussion will be of greater benefit to the individual than simply distributing holy communion to everyone present.

This also brings up the point that just because people are ill or elderly does not mean that they are sinless, or are unable to sin in the future. Occasionally ask them if they would like the priest to come that week for the Sacrament of Reconciliation, or the Anointing of the Sick, especially if it seems to the minister that a person is seriously ill.

Why can't we give holy communion to non-Catholics indiscriminately, without worrying about fulfilling those conditions?

This is a very sensitive question, particularly when someone who does not know our tradition is hurt when we refuse. This can happen when the question is asked before a wedding or funeral, or when a special minister is visiting someone's house. To give the correct answer, and to explain it sympathetically, requires some preparation.

Holy communion is very important to us, both as the Body and Blood of Christ, and as the sign of our shared faith as Catholic Christians. The Catholic Church, unlike some of the Protestant Churches, has never practiced "an open table," inviting one and all to receive. In fact, we have been extraordinarily strict even with ourselves, demanding that the communicant be free from mortal sin and adhere to certain rules of fasting. While we are taught to speak of communion as our necessary food, we also see it as privilege. For a Catholic to receive holy communion is to vouch that all is substantially well with one's personal relationships with God and his Church. If things are not well—if one has substantially violated God's love and/or the community's morality—then tradition tells one not to approach the altar until after sacramental reconciliation.

Despite our democratic sentiments, or fear of giving offense, we should realize that giving holy communion indiscriminately is not part of our tradition at all, and that the state of grace is essential for the people who seek this sacrament. "Holy things for holy people!" is one of the ancient exclamatory warnings at the eucharist given by the deacon before distribution of the Body and Blood. Catholics must be well-prepared, and non-Catholics must have a true justification. Paragraph no. 21 of the Instruction, "Concerning Cases When Other Christians May Be Admitted to Eucharistic Communion in the Catholic Church," reiterates: "Of its very nature celebration of the Eucharist signifies the fullness of profession of faith and the fullness of ecclesial communion. This principle must not be obscured and must remain our guide in this field."

Suppose someone whom I know is not a Catholic comes up to me at Mass to receive the host or drink from the chalice. What should I do?

You should act with discretion and charity. You should not disturb the congregation or embarrass the individual. Later on, you alert your pastor to what occurred, and/or speak to the person yourself. But at that moment, you should give the person Holy Communion, for certain reasons you will appreciate: you could be wrong, and in the process, embarrass someone greatly; right or wrong about the person's affiliation, people in the congregation often notice these encounters and think we are humiliating someone; no one, not even a priest, totally knows the heart of another; there could be occasions when a person is convinced that this is the right thing for him/her to do; later on, the facts of the matter can be established; if that person *is* receiving when he/she should not do so, it is most often through ignorance, and a friendly conversation in private will be a much more respectful technique than a shake of the head and a whispered, "You can't receive."

Whether you think you know the situation or not, remember that no one is supposed to ask a Catholic if he or she is in the state of grace when that person approaches the altar; suspicion and challenge are foreign to that sacred moment.

This is not to ignore the situation. Repeated reception through ignorance is nothing we should tolerate. And in fact, there is a recent statement about this from the United States Catholic Bishops that you should study yourself and show to others when there is confusion. By order of our Bishops, as of November, 1986, it is now being included in all American liturgical aids, such as missalettes. The full text is given here:

GUIDELINES FOR RECEIVING COMMUNION

For Catholics
Catholics fully participate in the celebration of the Eucharist when they receive Holy Communion in fulfillment of Christ's command to eat His Body and drink His Blood. In order to be properly disposed to receive Communion, communicants should not be conscious of grave sin, have fasted for an hour, and seek to live in charity and love with their neighbors. Persons conscious of grave sin must first be reconciled with God and the Church through the sacrament of Penance. A frequent reception of the sacrament of Penance is encouraged for all.

For Other Christians

We welcome to this celebration of the Eucharist those
Christians who are not fully united with us. It is a
consequence of the sad divisions in Christianity that we
cannot extend to them a general invitation to receive
Communion. Catholics believe that the Eucharist is an
action of the celebrating community signifying a oneness
in faith, life, and worship of the community. Reception of
the Eucharist by Christians not fully united with us would
imply a oneness which does not yet exist, and for which
we must all pray.

For Those Not Receiving Communion

Those not receiving sacramental Communion are
encouraged to express in their hearts a prayerful desire for
unity with the Lord Jesus and with one another.

For Non-Christians

We also welcome to this celebration those who do not
share our faith in Jesus. While we cannot extend to them
an invitation to receive Communion, we do invite them to
be united with us in prayer.

Appendix I

The Rite of Commissioning Special Ministers of Holy Communion

1. Persons authorized to distribute holy communion in special circumstances should be commissioned by the local Ordinary or his delegate[1] according to the following rite. The rite should take place in the presence of the people during Mass or outside Mass.

A. DURING MASS

2. In the homily the celebrant first explains the reason for this ministry and then presents to the people those chosen to serve as special ministers, using these or similar words:
Dear friends in Christ,
Our brothers and sisters N.* and N. are to be entrusted with administering the eucharist, with taking communion to the sick, and with giving it as viaticum to the dying.

The celebrant pauses, and then addresses the candidates:
In this ministry, you must be examples of Christian living in faith and conduct; you must strive to grow in holiness through this sacrament of unity and love. Remember that, though many, we are one body because we share the one bread and one cup.

As ministers of holy communion be, therefore, especially observant of the Lord's command to love your neighbor. For when he gave his body as food to his disciples, he said to them: "This is my commandment, that you should love one another as I have loved you."

3. After the address the candidates stand before the celebrant, who asks them these questions:
Are you resolved to undertake the office of giving the body and blood of the Lord to your brothers and sisters, and so serve to build up the Church?
℟. **I am.**

Are you resolved to administer the holy eucharist with the utmost care and reverence?
℟. **I am.**

4. All stand. The candidates kneel and the celebrant invites the faithful to pray:
Dear friends in Christ,
Let us pray with confidence to the Father; let us ask him to bestow his blessings on our brothers and sisters, chosen to be ministers of the eucharist.

Pause for silent prayer. The celebrant then continues:
Merciful Father,
creator and guide of your family,
bless ✠ our brothers and sisters N and N.

May they faithfully give the bread of life
to your people.

Strengthened by this sacrament,
may they come at last
to the banquet of heaven.

We ask this through Christ our Lord.
℟. Amen.

5. The general intercessions should include an intention for the newly-commissioned ministers.

6. In the procession at the presentation of gifts. the newly-commissioned ministers carry the vessels with the bread and wine, and at communion may receive the eucharist under both kinds.

B. OUTSIDE MASS

7. When the people are assembled an appropriate song is sung. The celebrant greets the people. There normally follows a short liturgy of the Word. The readings and chants are taken, either in whole or in part, from the liturgy of the day or from those listed in the ritual.

8. The rite continues as above, nos. 2-5.

9. Finally, the celebrant blesses the people and dismisses them in the usual way. The rite concludes with an appropriate song.

[1]See instruction *Immensae caritatis* I, nos. 1, 6.

* This reference may be modified according to circumstances.

Appendix II

Administration of Communion to the Sick by a Special Minister

The texts in italics are Father Belford's personal comments on each part of the rite. In services of this kind, a certain amount of flexibility and creativity on the part of the special minister will make the prayer experience more satisfying for everyone.

COMMUNION IN ORDINARY CIRCUMSTANCES

PASTORAL NOTES

This rite is for use of a special minister of the eucharist when communion can be celebrated in the context of a liturgy of the word. Since some options pertaining to priests and deacons alone have been eliminated in this booklet, those ministers should use the complete ritual book, *Pastoral Care of the Sick: Rites of Anointing and Viaticum.*

Priests with pastoral responsibilities should see to it that the sick or aged, even though not seriously ill or in danger of death, are given every opportunity to receive the eucharist frequently, even daily, especially during the Easter season. They may receive communion at any hour. Those who care for the sick may receive communion with them, in accord with the usual norms. To provide frequent communion for the sick, it may be necessary to ensure that the community has a sufficient number of ministers of communion. The communion minister should wear attire appropriate to the ministry.

The sick person and others may help to plan the celebration, for example, by choosing the prayers and readings. Those making these choices should keep in mind the condition of the sick person. The readings and the homily should help those present to reach a deeper understanding of the mystery of human suffering in relation to the paschal mystery of Christ.

The faithful who are ill are deprived of their rightful and accustomed place in the eucharistic community. In bringing communion to them the minister of communion represents Christ and manifests faith and charity on behalf of the whole community toward those who cannot be present at the eucharist. For the sick the reception of communion is not only a privilege but also a sign of support and concern shown by the Christian community for its members who are ill.

The links between the community's eucharistic celebration, especially on the Lord's Day, and the communion of the sick are intimate and manifold. Besides remembering the sick in the general intercessions at Mass, those present should be reminded occasionally of the significance of communion in the lives of those who are ill: union with Christ in his struggle with evil, his prayer for the world, and his love for the Father, and union with the community from which they are separated.

The obligation to visit and comfort those who cannot take part in the eucharistic assembly may be clearly demonstrated by taking communion to them from the community's eucharistic celebration. This symbol of unity between the community and its sick members has the deepest significance on the Lord's Day, the special day of the eucharistic assembly.

When the eucharist is brought to the sick, it should be carried in a pyx or small closed container. Those who are with the sick should be asked to prepare a table covered with a linen cloth upon which the blessed sacrament will be placed. Lighted candles are prepared and, where it is customary, a vessel of holy water. Care should be taken to make the occasion special and joyful.

Sick people who are unable to receive communion under the form of bread may receive it under the form of wine alone. If the wine is consecrated at a Mass not celebrated in the presence of the sick person, the blood of the Lord is kept in a properly covered vessel and is placed in the tabernacle after communion. The precious blood should be carried to the sick in a vessel which is closed in such a way as to eliminate all danger of spilling. If some of the precious blood remains, it should be consumed by the minister, who should also see to it that the vessel is properly purified.

If the sick wish to celebrate the sacrament of penance, it is preferable that a priest make himself available for this during a previous visit.

INTRODUCTORY RITES

When the special minister enters the home or apartment of the sick person, they can greet one another in their usual friendly way. When all people present are ready to begin the communion service, the minister gives the liturgical greeting (e.g., "Peace be with this house and with all who live here"). Then the minister takes the pyx containing the eucharist out of pocket or purse and places it on the clean cloth on a table that has been prepared with candles and a crucifix. The pyx should be visible to everyone. After the greeting, the minister invites the sick person and all present to recall and repent of their sins. The rite offers several options which can be alternated from time to time.

GREETING
The minister greets the sick person and the others present. One of the following may be used:
The peace of the Lord be with you always.
People: **And also with you.**

Or:
Peace be with you (this house) and with all who live here.

Or:
The grace of our Lord Jesus Christ and the love of God and the fellowship of the Holy Spirit be with you all.

Or:
The grace and peace of God our Father and the Lord Jesus Christ be with you.

The minister then places the blessed sacrament on the table and all join in adoration.

PENITENTIAL RITE
The minister invites the sick person and all present to join in the penitential rite, using these or similar words:
My brothers and sisters, to prepare ourselves for this celebration, let us call to mind our sins.

Or:
My brothers and sisters, let us turn with confidence to the Lord and ask his forgiveness for all our sins.

After a brief period of silence, the penitential rite continues, using one of the following:
Lord Jesus, you healed the sick:
Lord, have mercy.
People: **Lord, have mercy.**

Lord Jesus, you forgave sinners:
Christ, have mercy.
People: **Christ, have mercy.**

Lord Jesus, you give us yourself to heal us and bring us strength:
Lord, have mercy.
People: **Lord, have mercy.**

Or all say:
I confess to almight God,
and to you, my brothers and sisters,
that I have sinned through my own fault

They strike their breast.

in my thoughts and in my words,
in what I have done,
and in what I have failed to do;
and I ask blessed Mary, ever virgin,
all the angels and saints,
and you, my brothers and sisters,
to pray for me to the Lord our God.

The minister concludes the penitential rite with the following:

May almighty God have mercy on us,
forgive us our sins,
and bring us to everlasting life.
People: **Amen.**

LITURGY OF THE WORD

After the penitential rite, the minister introduces this part of the service with an invitation such as, "Let us now open our hearts to take guidance and comfort from the holy Word of God."

The scripture readings should be proclaimed from a ritual text prepared for the special minister or a Bible (either the communicant's or the minister's) or from an official liturgical book such as the Lectionary. Responsibility for lectoring could certainly be shared among those present.

The minister may choose one of the short scripture passages printed below or a longer passage selected from Pastoral Care of the Sick: Rites of Anointing and Viaticum. *While these passages, and also the accounts of the passion of the Lord, are particularly recommended for the consolation of the sick, the minister is not limited only to these parts of the Bible. In fact, especially if the communicant is not newly sick, and has already begun to understand the mystery of the cross present in every life, it would be advisable for the minister to proclaim the same scripture readings that the universal church is hearing on that particular day. In all cases the scripture readings should be done in a reverent but relaxed way: seated unless everyone is able and desires to stand for the Gospel. Whenever possible the proper introductory and concluding formulas should be used.*

READING

The word of God is proclaimed by one of those present or by the minister. A reading assigned for the day in the *Lectionary for Mass* or one of the following readings may be used:

John 6:51
Jesus says:
"I myself am the living bread
come down from heaven.
If anyone eats this bread

he shall live forever;
the bread I will give
is my flesh, for the life of the whole world."

John 6:54–58
Jesus says:
"He who feeds on my flesh
and drinks my blood
has life eternal,
and I will raise him up on the last day.
For my flesh is real food
and my blood real drink.
The man who feeds on my flesh
and drinks my blood
remains in me, and I in him.
Just as the Father who has life sent me
and I have life because of the Father,
so the man who feeds on me
will have life because of me.
This is the bread that came down from heaven.
Unlike your ancestors who ate and died nonetheless,
the man who feeds on this bread shall live forever."

John 14:6
Jesus says:
"I am the way, and the truth, and the life;
no one comes to the Father but through me."

John 15:5
Jesus says:
"I am the vine, you are the branches.
He who lives in me and I in him,
will produce abundantly,
for apart from me you can do nothing."

1 John 4:16
We have come to know and to believe
in the love God has for us.
God is love,
and he who abides in love
abides in God,
and God in him.

1 Kings 19:4–8   God strengthens and comforts his servants.
Job 19:23–27a   I know that my Redeemer lives.
Wisdom 9:1, 9–18   Who could know your counsel? We ask to share in God's wisdom.
Isaiah 35:1–10   Strengthen the feeble hands.
Isaiah 52:13–53:12   He bore our sufferings himself.

Acts 3:1–10   In the name of Jesus, stand up and walk.
Acts 4:8–12   There is no other name by which we are able to be saved.
Romans 8:18–27   We groan while we wait for the redemption of our bodies. The Spirit enables us to pray in our suffering.
Romans 8:31b–35, 37–39   Nothing can come between us and the love of Christ.
1 Corinthians 1:18–25   God's weakness is stronger than human strength.
1 Corinthians 15:12–20   Christ has been raised from the dead; through him has come the resurrection of us all.
James 5:13–16   This prayer, made in faith, will save the sick person.

Matthew 5:1–12a   Rejoice and be glad, for your reward is great in heaven.
Matthew 8:5–17   He bore our infirmities.
Mark 2:1–12   Seeing their faith, Jesus said to the sick man: Your sins are forgiven.
Mark 10:46–52   Jesus, Son of David, have mercy on me.
Luke 10:25–37   Who is my neighbor?
Luke 11:5–13   Ask and it will be given to you.
John 6:53–58   Whoever eats this bread has eternal life.
John 10:11–18   The good shepherd lays down his life for his sheep.

See *Pastoral Care of the Sick: Rites of Anointing and Viaticum* or the *Lectionary for Mass* for a further selection of texts.

RESPONSE
A brief period of silence may be observed after the reading of the word of God. The minister may then give a brief explanation of the reading, applying it to the needs of the sick person and those who are looking after him or her.

The general intercessions may be said. With a brief
introduction the minister invites all those present to pray.
After the intentions the minister says the concluding prayer.
It is desirable that the intentions be announced by someone
other than the minister.

LITURGY OF HOLY COMMUNION

*Having met the Lord in his word, the sick person is ready now to
meet him in his sacrament.*

THE LORD'S PRAYER

The minister introduces the Lord's Prayer in these or similar
  words:
Now let us pray as Christ the Lord has taught us:

Or:
**And now let us pray with confidence as Christ our Lord
commanded:**

All say:
Our Father . . .

COMMUNION

The minister shows the eucharistic bread to those present,
saying:
This is the bread of life.
Taste and see that the Lord is good.

Or:
**This is the Lamb of God
who takes away the sins of the world.
Happy are those who are called to his supper.**

The sick person and all who are to receive communion say:
**Lord, I am not worthy to receive you,
but only say the word and I shall be healed.**

The minister goes to the sick person and, showing the
blessed sacrament, says:
The body of Christ.
The sick person answers: "Amen," and receives
communion. Then the minister says:

The blood of Christ.
The sick person answers: "Amen," and receives communion. Others present who wish to receive communion then do so in the usual way. After the conclusion of the rite, the minister cleanses the vessel as usual.

SILENT PRAYER
Then a period of silence may be observed.

A period of silent or verbal thanksgiving follows before the minister selects and offers the concluding prayer. The minister should be directive and not allow other conversations to start or distractions to take place. Three texts are given below. In every instance the minister begins by saying: **Let us pray.**

PRAYER AFTER COMMUNION
The minister says a concluding prayer. One of the following may be used:
Let us pray.

Pause for silent prayer, if this has not preceded.

**God our Father,
you have called us to share the one bread and one cup
and so become one in Christ.**

**Help us to live in him
that we may bear fruit,
rejoicing that he has redeemed the world.**

We ask this through Christ our Lord.
People: **Amen.**

Or:
**All-powerful God,
we thank you for the nourishment you give us
through your holy gift.**

**Pour out your Spirit upon us
and in the strength of this food from heaven
keep us single-minded in your service.**

We ask this in the name of Jesus the Lord.

Or:
All-powerful and ever-living God,
may the body and blood of Christ your Son
be for our brother/sister N.
a lasting remedy for body and soul.

We ask this through Christ our Lord.

CONCLUDING RITE

BLESSING
The minister invokes God's blessing and makes the sign of
the cross on himself or herself, while saying:

May the Lord bless us,
protect us from all evil,
and bring us to everlasting life.
People: **Amen.**

Or:
May the almighty and merciful God bless and protect us,
the Father, and the Son, ✠ and the Holy Spirit.

IN A HOSPITAL OR NURSING HOME

In a hospital or nursing facility the people who wish to receive
holy communion should be invited and helped to gather in one
place for a communion service, just as they gather periodically
for Mass. Under these circumstances a special minister can
celebrate the Ordinary Rite of Communion of the Sick.
Afterwards the minister might visit the remaining patients or
residents in their rooms and celebrate the Short Rite.

When ministers have to go from room to room, they face the
special challenge of being personal and prayerful over and over
again, and must try to avoid any impression of being perfunctory,
abrupt, or uninterested in the person they are with. This is
difficult, but it is important to the communicant to have prayerful
contact with another believer greater than the mere swift giving
of the host.

One suggestion for the eucharistic minister would be this model,
which emphasizes personal identification and shared prayer. The

*minister might enter the person's room with a greeting such as,
"Peace be with you, _____," or, "_____, may the peace of the
Lord be always with you." Then the minister says, "I am _____
from Holy Family Parish," or, "I am _____, a special minister of
the eucharist helping Fr. Jones, the chaplain." "You are now
about to receive the Lord of your life, the risen savior who has
power over sin and sickness. To prepare for you to receive the
Lord Jesus in holy communion, let us pray the Our Father
together . . ." The minister continues with the "Lamb of God".*

*Through experience each special minister will find other ways
to approach the bedridden. The basic ritual under these
circumstances is Communion in a Hospital or Institution.*

COMMUNION IN A HOSPITAL OR INSTITUTION

INTRODUCTORY RITE

ANTIPHON
The rite may begin in the church, the hospital chapel, or the
first room, where the minister says one of the following
antiphons:
**How holy this feast
in which Christ is our food:
his passion is recalled;
grace fills our hearts;
and we receive a pledge of the glory to come.**

Or:
**How gracious you are, Lord:
your gift of bread from heaven
reveals a Father's love and brings us perfect joy.
You fill the hungry with good things
and send the rich away empty.**

Or:
**I am the living bread
come down from heaven.
If you eat this bread
you will live for ever.**

**The bread I will give is my flesh
for the life of the world.**

If it is customary, the minister may be accompanied by a
person carrying a candle.

LITURGY OF HOLY COMMUNION

GREETING
On entering each room, the minister may use one of the
greetings provided in the rite of Communion in Ordinary
Circumstances (p. 54). The minister then places the blessed
sacrament on the table, and all join in adoration. If there is
time and it seems desirable, the minister may proclaim a
Scripture reading from those found on pages 56–58.

THE LORD'S PRAYER
When circumstances permit (for example, when there are not
many rooms to visit), the minister is encouraged to lead the
sick in the Lord's Prayer. The minister introduces the Lord's
Prayer in these or similar words:
**Jesus taught us to call God our Father, and so we have the
courage to say:**

Or:
Now let us pray as Christ the Lord has taught us:

All say:
Our Father . . .

COMMUNION
The minister shows the eucharistic bread to those present,
saying:
**This is the Lamb of God
who takes away the sins of the world.
Happy are those who hunger and thirst,
for they shall be satisfied.**

Or:
**This is the bread of life,
Taste and see that the Lord is good.**
The rite then continues as described on page 59.

CONCLUDING RITE

CONCLUDING PRAYER

The concluding prayer may be said either in the last room visited, in the church, or chapel. One of the prayers given in the rite of Communion in Ordinary Circumstances (pp. 60–61) may be used. The blessing is omitted and the minister cleanses the vessel as usual.